# *Life Of An Artist Something From Nothing*

# Life Of An Artist Something From Nothing

*A book about experiences*

## KARUN S. PRAKASH

*Life Of An Artist Something From Nothing*

Copyright © 2022 by Karun S. Prakash. All rights reserved.

No part of this publication may be reproduced, stored in a retrieval system or transmitted in any way by any means, electronic, mechanical, photocopy, recording or otherwise without the prior permission of the author except as provided by USA copyright law.

The opinions expressed by the author are not necessarily those of URLink Print and Media.

1603 Capitol Ave., Suite 310 Cheyenne, Wyoming USA 82001
1-888-980-6523 | admin@urlinkpublishing.com

URLink Print and Media is committed to excellence in the publishing industry.

Book design copyright © 2022 by URLink Print and Media. All rights reserved.

Published in the United States of America
ISBN 978-1-68486-326-6 (Paperback)
ISBN 978-1-68486-329-7 (Digital)

24.10.22

# Table of Contents

- Introduction .................................................................................. 7
- Foreword ..................................................................................... 11
- Hope ........................................................................................... 15
- Corporate Mindset ...................................................................... 19
- Understanding Yourself .............................................................. 23
- Fear and Failure .......................................................................... 27
- Breaking the Habit ..................................................................... 31
- Inspiration .................................................................................. 35
- Opportunity ................................................................................ 39
- A Moment for Love .................................................................... 43
- Meeting with Leaders ................................................................. 47
- Entrepreneurs' Speeches ............................................................. 51
- The Gift You Are Given ............................................................. 55
- Knowledge .................................................................................. 59
- Learning Respect from Disrespect .............................................. 63
- Moments of Losing Everything .................................................. 67
- The Words .................................................................................. 71
- When Others Feel Pity for You .................................................. 75
- Ways of Funding Without Getting Funded ................................. 79
- Working on a Very High Level ................................................... 83
- Self-Awareness / Be Patient ....................................................... 87
- Self-Motivation .......................................................................... 91
- Feeling of Being Alone ............................................................... 95
- Won't Matter if I Left ................................................................. 99
- Photography & Writing .............................................................. 103

# Introduction

This book is inspired by true events and my journey of self-understanding and of life. It is inspired by my experiences and understanding of awareness, not knowing how to read or write, and being looked down on by others as a person who will never be successful. By understanding the ailments of life and being thankful for a second chance to make things happen in life. And by not having friends in life, being humble and strong to help others, and still going after my dreams. I have come a long way to share this story of my life and of being thankful in many ways.

One thing I've learned is that being successful in life does not happen by earning money but by earning others' respect, by working hard with people, helping others to never give up, and appreciating every small thing in life. I was inspired by hard work, my parents' hard work, and the support of my mom and my sister. Working hard, being patient, being humble, and just being a person that is inspired by leaders, speakers, mentors, and most importantly, just being myself. I hope you enjoy this book that I wrote about seeing this beautiful life and being inspired by arts, music, food, people with big hearts, and magazine articles.

Thank you all for taking the time to read my book. I hope this book inspires you in some way.

Many thanks,<br>
Karun S. Prakash<br>
Author

# I
# FOREWORD

# Foreword

I was born on March 3, 1983, in the small town of Tamavua in Fiji. I really don't remember much about it, but what I can tell you about my life is that it took hard work to believe in myself and understand what life is, and to give back to those who needed it the most. My life changed at the age of five. After that, I didn't know what I was going to be, what I was going to do, or how I was going to do it. I remember being on the bus with my mom and my baby sister, Lorin, on our way home from the hospital. I remember being happy, looking out the window with the wind blowing on my face and enjoying life as we waited for the bus to stop near the street across from my big, blue house. Before I knew it, the bus came to a stop. I was so excited that I jumped out of my seat and ran outside while my mom was carrying my little sister in her arms. When I got off the bus, I saw my house right across the street, and I started to think that if I ran really fast to cross the street, I could make it all the way. I heard my mom calling me by my nickname, Bunty. She told me to wait and that she was coming. Meanwhile, I was still thinking that I could make it across the street. I walked in front of the bus to see if there were any cars driving by, but there was a moment of silence. Like, there was not even a bit of wind. While my mom was still getting off the bus, I moved back a bit from the front of the bus and counted to three. Then, I ran as fast as I could, knowing in my mind that I would still be able to make it. As I darted across the street, out of nowhere, a minivan the size of a U.S. mail van hit me while going 25 to 35 miles per hour. My mom and the bus driver watched me fly through the air and land on the side of the street, like I was doll. I lay there for a minute and then got up. I looked at my hands covered in blood. I felt my face and saw my arms – half of my body was covered in blood. I looked up to find my mom, and when I did, I fainted. But before I blacked out, I did hear an ambulance. When I opened my eyes that night, I saw all my family, including the ones from Australia. Getting hit by a van put me in the newspaper, not only in Fiji, but also in the Australian news. So, fast forward, one asks how my life changed after that. I couldn't read, write, or spell. I even had seizures and asthma attacks; my sister was there for me every time I fell and started to shake. I dropped hot water on my legs and was at the hospital every month. I couldn't go back to school, and my mom was stressed out. She didn't know how she was going to make it in life, but she never gave up hope. Going forward, I came to the United States of America in June of 1995 at the age of eleven. Not knowing anyone and starting anew with everything was a bit hard. On top of that, I still didn't even know how to read or write. Nevertheless, I attended Martin Luther King Jr. Middle School from the age of 11 to 14 and did graduate. I really don't know how I did it, but I did do it. After graduating middle school, I went to Seaside High School. At the age of 15, I still didn't know how to read and write, but some things started to make sense.

I was made fun of and bullied just because I didn't know how to read or write or fit in with all the other so-called cool kids, but deep down inside, I was strong, and I believed in myself. I kept telling myself that one day I'd know how to read and write.

Joining high school, I had a hard time doing everything. I knew I had to keep trying and giving my best. I remember there was one night when I was driving home from a dinner party at Pebble Beach, and I stopped at a red light and was waiting for the light to turn green so I could go home to see my family. As I waited, my car was suddenly getting hit left and right with gunshots. I was at the wrong place at the wrong time. My car was riddled with bullet holes on the driver's side front and rear doors, but nothing happened to me. I was lucky to be alive.

Going back to the story, during my last year of high school before graduating, I started reading my first book, *Harvard Business Review on The Mind of the Leader*, and I earned a GPA of 3.83. I was so happy because I not only graduated from high school, but I also got into Monterey Peninsula College (MPC) as well. Right after my two years at MPC, I got into Art Institute of Hollywood in Los Angeles, California. I majored in Fashion Design & Arts. After college in LA, within the next two years, I found out that my mom and dad were getting divorced and that would leave my mom and my sister with financial problems.

I transferred colleges back to Monterey to help my mom and my sister with the financials. After finishing my major at MPC with a GPA of 4.0 and being awarded with a certificate in Fashion Design in the year 2009, I founded a company at the age of 27 called Shashi Clothing LLC. Long story short, the company didn't even last 4 years. It was like a car that didn't start. However, because of closing the company, I learned a lot, like how to start from the basic level of an idea and make it stronger.

I founded KSP & DESIGN CO. at age 32 on August 5, 2015. Now, this was a company with the same concept but a better-formed business idea. I knew I was going to push this all the way to make it happen, no matter what stood in my way. Let me tell you, it feels really good to come back strong. With KSP & DESIGN CO., I did decide to close this company as well, but I kept the skills and the idea of the business while still pushing forward with my photography website that I also had at the same time I ran the online fashion company. To date, I still have very successful opportunities with new clients, including photoshoots and pitching ideas for fashion ads.

# II
# HOPE

# Hope

What is hope to me? It is keeping myself alive every day and telling myself that the day will come when I can tell everyone about my life and share with the world how you really can be whatever you want to be and make a difference. Making a difference in life is what you do to change the world and how much you give to those who are where you used to be when you were trying to get somewhere in life. That's what I did. I just looked deep inside myself and told myself that, one day, I will be someone, and I won't stop until my time is up. I remember how I met so many people who said they believed in me, but deep down, I could read them so well to the point where I just wanted to walk away from every word they said that made it seem like they really cared.

I had so many of these moments in my life that it just almost made me sick. The worst part was talking to someone about the business, and they would say things like, "This is high-fashion, and I know what I'm talking about," while sitting in a boxed showroom where the clothing looked outdated, and the garments needed to go back to where they came from. I remember having meeting after meeting, and the people I met would say that they would help me with this and that. Their promises were an oh-my-God-is-this-really-going-to-happen moment that made me get my hopes up. But then, I realize and think, *Really?! Like, shit, I almost believed that.*

As I was saying, you must look deep down within yourself and ask, "Who am I? What am I going to be or do right?" You must gain balance in your life, starting with your mind, your soul, your Self, the moment you are in, and where you are going. It happened to me one day, and I told myself there are no 'ifs' – it just must happen, and it will happen. What does this have to do with hope? Everything! You see, in life, you must believe in yourself, in what you want, and in where you are going – and that is hope.

Having hope gives you a key to remember and follow to open your mind to something that you're trying to be. Hope gives you a key to where you want to go, which will take you to your first step in opening your eyes and seeing your path to success and where you want to go five years from now. You see, having hope with a clear mind gives you a roadmap for you to start and to not have to wait for whatever reason you're holding back. With hope, there is no one, I mean, no one stopping you but YOU. So, what are you waiting for? Christmas?

# III

# CORPORATE MINDSET

# Corporate Mindset

After my great daily morning workout, I check my schedule in my iPad to see what's planned for the day. I am dressed in a white dress shirt with nice, fitted pants and a black skinny tie, and I top it off with a black, fitted sports coat, a brown belt, and shoes.

After reading everything on my schedule for the day, I get my Chai tea ready to get me going for the morning. Every businessperson has either a newspaper or apps on their go-to device to read through their daily business news that helps keep up their productivity for the day. I check LinkedIn or Pulse for the news to keep up with the daily headlines and to have an understanding of what I'm going to do that day. You see, to make or plot a roadmap for your company, you need to understand what is going on every day for you to know which path you are going to take in the long run. Most businesspeople like me are busy with our work and feel that twenty-four hours is not enough; we wish we had more time. An understanding of yourself, your mind, and your self-management is a way to keep up with everyone around you. Every corporate mindset is a level of understanding, and you must see your surroundings with yourself and with your business.

Partnership is important. It's very important to have someone as a second eye, being there for you every step of the way. It's like your cell phone. It is with you wherever you go, but at this point, you can keep your privacy with your businessperson; your cell phone knows everything about you! If you're thinking of becoming someone, don't wait. Time is too short, and you have no time to waste. Instead, plan and understand where you want to go. Ask yourself if it's right for you, if it's what you really want to do, or if it fits for where you want to be in the next five years.

You as a person need to know what you really want because if you are going to own your own company, then let me give you this wake-up call. Owning a company and doing business with other companies out there is no joke, and you cannot walk around and say that you founded a company and this is what it's going to do. If this is what you're thinking, you already lost in becoming a business owner, and don't even think about owning something big unless you really understand it from your heart. Wake up every morning, and think about your company every day of your life until you really become that person. The key to all of this is just the beginning of your personal corporate mindset. Good Luck.

# IV

# UNDERSTANDING YOURSELF

# Understanding Yourself

Self-understanding is how you hold yourself together – meaning don't worry so much about what others are saying, but free your mind to be on your own path. Now, you see, everyone and every person has a dream – to be somebody when they grow up. But not everyone follows through with self-understanding. If you're thinking of starting a company or business, then you need to not only listen to what other business owners are telling you, but you also need to relay to others what you're saying about yourself. Neophytes out there may ask how you think about so many things at one time, right? So, you see, everyone out there thinks too much, and they think it's their job to do so when really, you're just relaying what you really want to do or say to someone. You not only can apply this to your life on a day-to-day basis, but also to the company that you're trying to start. Remember that you can only do this by understanding yourself.

Understanding yourself is easy, and fun in a way, because you only do and think about the things that you really want. To do this, you must really think deep down inside about what you really want from life and for yourself, your family, and everyone that you love.

Things can wait. For most people, it is easy to say "Yes, I can try it" today, but tomorrow we'll see, right? That is because they and everyone else gives up so easily in life that they forget about the things they really want to do. Now, before people can even begin to think about starting their own business, they are happy to talk about their ideas for starting something and making a difference to help others, right? However, the idea is only an idea, and it's going to stay with you only for that day or maybe not even half a day because you're already thinking about a thousand other things that you really want to do even more than starting your own company and sticking to that one idea to make it happen.

You see, in the business world today, entrepreneurs don't have twenty-four hours in a day to do everything that they want. Twenty-four hours is like five minutes in a whole day for business owners who are always on the go and in pursuit of something that they believe in, and the ideas that they come up with and follow through with. And in those moments they know they must spend less time thinking (and more time doing) but also think out of the box to stay on that path of success for their company. You attract only what you want; you spend time thinking about only what you want. Go after only what you want, and believe in the idea that you came up with to help you understand yourself.

# V

# FEAR AND FAILURE

# Fear and Failure

All of us have fears in life about something, but we try our best to keep moving forward. Fear of trying to get there, fear of making it happen, fear of walking alone, and fear of your own dreams. Now, if fear is where you are, then let's not even talk about failure. As humans, we are very absent-minded in everyday life, and we are so distracted in things that we forget about the life that we really want to have. Fear is nothing. It does not even exist, because fear is only in your head. But this fear in your head is deterring you from trying new things and moving on with life.

You fear failure and trying new things, but you don't even know what will happen if you do try. I had a hard time thinking about these words *fear* and *failure*. I had a hard time with giving up and trying new things in life, because I was thinking about what others would think of my idea and whether they would make fun of me for trying. You see, as you go along with life, you tend to have all these ideas in your head, and you can only talk about it to yourself. You're too afraid of showing your ideas and your art and yourself to others, because you don't know how to. That is where I used to be in life, and the funny part about all this is that, when I'm in the shower thinking about an idea, I tend to talk about it as if I was in front of an investor or at a board meeting in my own company, and I'd be on the go like there was no tomorrow! I went on about my idea and with my speech, and I'm feeling great because I'm helping those people. Giving them advice on how to start a company and to make them understand that becoming someone in life means you are trying your best to live that life and the dream that you always wanted. I was super motivated in the speech I was giving to my imaginary audience, and I am proud of myself and the leader that I am in life. I get to live my dream and help others in life because of where I came from and how hard I tried. All this happened in the shower with my eyes closed, and as soon as I opened my eyes, I was like, *Man, reality sucks!* The only thing that I got from that was an empty room and a huge water bill.

We all have fears inside of us, and yes, sometimes, we all must think twice about some things in life. But fear is not helpful when you feel paralyzed and don't want to do anything about your life, and you just want to move on from not thinking about the life that you one day wished you had and the dream that you always wanted. In life, we all have failed to do something we want or something that we think we can't have. The point is to not be afraid of fear and failure, because it's all just in your head, and there is nothing in life that you cannot do. You know that you can do whatever you want, and there is no human being that can stop you but you. So, as I'm saying, don't worry about the things in life, just make the most of it by caring about the small things that you have in life first. You are a very strong person, and you can have anything in life that you want. All you must do is be strong on the inside and believe in yourself and never give up. Fear and failure can take a walk on their own because there is no way in hell they can stop you from doing what you love.

# VI

# BREAKING THE HABIT

# Breaking the Habit

It's like an addiction to drugs or a habit that you can't seem to let go of, right? Well, there is one thing I want to help you understand: we humans are drawn to some things in life that makes us vulnerable and weak. Let's say your day starts off so well. From morning to almost mid-afternoon, you are on the go, and no one can stop you because it feels great to be in control of every moment of your time and be understanding of your space. But as you go along, you stop and think of that something that you should do because you think it won't hurt anyone if you just do it one more time, right? Well, think again. Right after you are drawn to that something or someone, that moment will last you just a short span of time that you won't care about as much because you have the habit of going to it repeatedly. In other words, you can forget about your loved ones because you are so drawn to your habits.

If you are a business owner, or trying to set your life on a road where you have a plan to move forward with your family and friends, and you seem to have these habits come along in your life much sooner than you think, and you can't really let go because you just love that feeling of being drawn to that bad habit, then this is for you. Your job is where you perform with your team and make them understand you from a business standpoint. Most of them won't really understand where you're coming from, because they haven't reached that mindset yet or they just don't really care about what you have to say for them to do their job right. Now, most commonly, when you have meetings as a leader and the face of the company, you lay down the rules not just for yourself, but also for your staff and the upcoming road to success. Some of your staff may be on their cell phones or talking to each other before the meeting starts, but when you walk into that room, every person in the room must welcome you by name and be ready to understand the points of their role and the overview of the meetings. The reason for the lack of enthusiasm may be that the staff has a particular habit of thinking to themselves, "Here goes another meeting," before going into the meeting. I understand where you are coming from because, to you, that company is your life, and you worked so hard to get there. If only your staff would understand the meaning of being professional.

It will drive you nuts in a way because they don't see what you see. To them, it's a habit of their mindset, a habit of saying something repeatedly. In other words, it may be the same agenda in the meetings, but overall, they are showing overconfidence in their mindset because, at the end of the day, even after attending the meetings, you find your staff making the same mistake over and over, and therefore, you do try your best to correct them and make them understand. It's the habits of your mindset, and you think your way through all these things and don't pay attention to yourself. A bad habit is where you do one thing repeatedly, and you are not seeing the outcome of your success. If you are in a customer service business, you want to make sure you are improving that skill. Having a bad habit is where you really don't care about what others are telling you and, in general, you are going to turn around and do it again and again because you find it easier to just follow the same habit.

# VII
# INSPIRATION

# Inspiration

Inspiration can come from anywhere, like yourself at one point in your life or even a person that you're in love with. My inspirations come from painting, music, a person singing, walking along with someone, and even just reading a book. Overall, you should be inspired by something to make you feel free and open-minded to help you be successful in your business or in life. Being inspired is the most beautiful thing in life, because it makes you want to do more and keeps you moving with everything you have in your mind.

Inspiration is something that we all are born with the power to feel, and the funniest part of all this is that we don't see it. We are so into ourselves and our thoughts about everyday life that we don't even think about being inspired by the things around us. We miss inspiration to make us who we are as a person or as an artist every day. Artists are living their lives every moment that they can; they are happy to be alive. Inspiration is so strong that it will keep you moving. In an artist's eyes, he or she sees the world as a playground, a place where they could see things that most people don't see. In an artist's eyes, he or she doesn't really need most of the tools in their hands to make things happen. They are born to make something that will stand out and make a difference in the world – a world where it's fun for everyone to enjoy moments before it's over.

The world is your sandbox, where you can begin to understand what life means and open the door that you want to open. Don't let anyone stop you, because this is you and your life – you will make something from the ground up. It's a blessing if you can see that because, in everyday life, not everyone will get to live their life the way they want to. Don't walk around and talk about what you're going to do – just go out there and make things happen. You see, my mind works just like music, where it creates a moment in writing and makes beats of sounds that no one has ever heard of yet. I walk in big, white, empty rooms and paints are just waiting for me to grab them. Music is playing in my head, and only I can hear it. The sound that I hear is like a ping from a piano with only one key and one note. A key with which I can write an album and more music without the piano. An artist has the power to change the world, not only with a voice, but also with their hands, creating a language without saying a word. You must be unseeing while seeing. An artist has a mind that keeps moving by doing many things at one time. You must be open-minded and see things that people won't understand. At some point, they will ask you what you see that they don't see, to understand you better. Being an artist is like being a part of a moving train. It will keep you going without any stop signs. The best thing about being an artist is their will to give and make things where they see and feel hope. They can use anything to make you understand the power of the mind and the soul of an artist by being the artist that they are. That's how I see life and everything around me – keep moving; the power I must make and see with the will I have to give is unstoppable. Every artist has their own circle within them, and only they can see it. So, go out there, and design from within, and give back to the world, because that's how you become a true artist.

# VIII
# OPPORTUNITY

# Opportunity

Most of us in life don't get an opportunity like others out there. Why? Because most of us are not the same as other people. What do I mean by that? I mean, look back to the beginning of this book where I talked about me not knowing how to read or write. When most people have an opportunity in life to become whatever they want, they let every opportunity go out the door because they don't value the moments in life. As mentioned in the previous chapters, I had to work very hard for what I have. I didn't even know how to read or write. So, it really did take a moment and lots of thinking about being in my shoes where I have this big dream to be someone, but I don't even know how to read or write! *How in the world am I going to do this?*

Most people who do get an opportunity in life to make something happen or to be someone don't really see how important that moment can be in their life, as well as their family's lives. You see, every day you lose moments in life to be someone, so why not try as hard as you can and make something out of it? Most kids, and even adults today, wish they had done something when they had the opportunity in life, but instead, they just didn't think it through as much at the time. Opportunity is as important as saving someone's life because it is usually a once-in-a-lifetime occurrence, so you grab that moment or just let it slip away from your hands.

Opportunity doesn't just sit there and wait while you're doing nothing at all to grab it. Nor does it wait while you talk about it repeatedly with your friends, saying that you have a great idea to be a successful person one day, but you're just talking way off your head and not doing anything about it. When you have an opportunity, just run for it. Don't think it through if you know it really feels great inside. That is your moment, and you should live it by feeling like you can do anything that you want to. You see, most of the people, when they do get an opportunity in life, would rather sit in one place and not do anything, because they think there is always tomorrow that they can do it, not knowing that the opportunity doesn't wait for you to make it happen. You have to get up and make it happen and make a difference in your own life.

You must grab your opportunity from inside your heart and run after it. Remember when you were a kid, and your mom and dad were trying to tell you not to do something because it wasn't right for them or you? Well, understanding your parents and hearing them out on what they're saying is one thing. Don't go yelling at your mom or dad or whoever. Just hear them out, because most of the time your mom and dad are trying to look after you and show you that all they want in life is the best moment for you where one day you can get that great opportunity of a lifetime. Look back to your mom and dad and thank them for showing you an opportunity where you were just trying to understand yourself. Thank you, mom and dad. I love you forever.

# IX

# A MOMENT FOR LOVE

# A Moment for Love

I know deep down inside that every woman wants to fall in love – a real love, where only you and that person can see the moment of love, and time is still. I once fell in love, and you know what the crazy part about all this is? After I saw her across the pool for the first time, I knew right away that I was in love. I mean, I forgot about everything that I was doing. I didn't even know how to talk to her or what to say. That moment felt so beautiful inside, and I just couldn't ask for anything else. Why? Because I knew at that moment that she was the one for me. As I was walking to the other side of the pool where she was playing with some kids and having fun and just enjoying the moment, I felt like everything in my life just went soft. All I wanted to do is just walk up next to her and look deep into her eyes and say, "I love you."

Don't you want to fall in love and forget about everything in that moment and just live your life filled with love and joy? Well, I do, and I would do anything for love, because we only get one chance to love and live that moment. I remember I felt so beautiful inside.

While I was looking at her, it started to rain, and I tell you, it was like a scene in one of the movies where everything is still, and you see only her and that's all. However, I lost the opportunity to say how I really felt about her, because she went off to college. I remember that day where I ran after her to the parking lot to tell her how I felt about her on the inside. I really wanted to just run after her, grab her hands, pull her close to me, look into her eyes, and tell her that I love her and that's how I really felt for her. I wanted to do all this before she was gone. Well, she was already gone, and when I got there, all I saw was an empty parking lot. It was a quiet moment with no sound nor wind. As teardrops fell, I looked up, opened my eyes, and tried to hold strong, knowing what just happened. But you know what? I didn't lose hope, and I didn't give up on what I believed in. When I saw her, I knew she was worth waiting for, for the rest of my life. If I had to wait, I would, because true love and those feelings only happen once in a lifetime.

There is a moment in your life when you just want to stop playing all the games, because it gets to the point where it doesn't matter anymore. Think about it, when you know from deep down inside that that's the person you really want to be with, and you are 100% sure that she is the one, why wait for it? You know, the best thing about life is that when you know it's right, then it's right. Don't worry about if she will say yes or no, because the best thing is just to talk to her and really tell her about how you feel deep inside your heart. She could listen to what you have to say, or she could be just like any other girl where she will just walk away while giving you a mean look. But overall, the best part about it is that you did tell her, and it doesn't matter if she said yes or no, because you told her how you really felt. That is what I did with the girl I talked about earlier, and the best part was that she took her time and listened to me and understood what I was telling her about how I felt and how much I wanted to be a part of her and her family's lives. If she gives me her time, there is nothing more I can ask for.

# X

# MEETING WITH LEADERS

# Meeting with Leaders

As an entrepreneur, you will meet lots of CEOs of other companies, and you will have to keep making connections in life if you're going to be serious about entrepreneurship. As I was becoming an entrepreneur, I got advice from many business owners and CEOs. I believe the best thing about this is that you are lucky to meet these people, so don't take it as it just being someone else. You are so lucky to meet them and to hear what they have to say about becoming a business owner or just being an entrepreneur. It's a big deal. So, you must feel it, believe it, and understand what they are telling you, because there is no such thing as knowing enough.

Being an entrepreneur, I keep my options open all the time. What I mean by that is, if I'm in a meeting hearing a CEO or some entrepreneurs speak, I take time to listen and understand what they are saying. Because as an entrepreneur, you will understand that you learn new things every day as you go along with your business. In the upcoming days before launching my fashion website, I met with two super nice businessmen that I happened to know at the Nicklaus Club Monterey, the place where I was working before launching my website.

One of the individuals is one of the nicest people I ever met in my life. Just to hear him speak about business and entrepreneurship was one of the biggest moments of my life. He told me about his ventures in life, his times of success and how he became a business entrepreneur, what it took for him to get this far in life with self-understanding, and how to look at things differently. In that moment, I understood where he was coming from, because although I did go to college to understand what I wanted to do, overall, most of my skills are self-taught. From that initial business conversation with him, he started giving me connections to some of the businesspeople and entrepreneurs he knew. He gave me the name of one of his entrepreneur friends – a President and CEO of a tech company. So, right after having a great meeting with one person, I went on to set up a call with another person on where to meet and what to talk about. This person and I ended up meeting at a Starbucks, one of the best places to meet someone for a great conversation.

Two minutes into the conversation and, I tell you, it was like the moment was right. I was thinking, *This guy knows how to have a conversation alright*. So, we went along talking about each other's business ventures and how each of us started our businesses. Listening to him talk really made me understand and be more motivated about what I was doing in my life as an entrepreneur. Talking to this person also made me understand that as an entrepreneur, you must keep moving in life. You must understand down which road you are driving your car and how far you must drive until you come to an end. So, by talking to this person, I started making connections from the information he knew that could help me with my upcoming life as a new entrepreneur in the business world. One of the key takeaways is: the more meetings you have, the more connections you will end up having in your upcoming days as an entrepreneur.

# XI

# ENTREPRENEURS' SPEECHES

# Entrepreneurs' Speeches

Speeches are one of the best ways to understand how entrepreneurs give their best in their business, as well as how they got started on their story. Yes, one of the best things that ever happened to me when I started to look up to Steve Jobs or even Tim Cook was to listen to them talk about how the Apple company keeps their mindset going. You see, for you to understand <u>how an entrepreneur is</u> means understanding their way of walking, talking, and meeting new people every day of their lives. So, for me to understand how and what made them go as entrepreneurs, and to understand myself on how and where I was going, and also why I was meeting all these new people that I didn't know about, all I wanted was just to ask questions about how to get started on my first stage of owning a business.

Researching business platforms, I got motivated on how I could hear all these businesspeople talk, see how they got started on their companies, and see how they balance life with how they move. But for me, I felt like, as much as I was trying to see who I was at the starting point of being an entrepreneur, something inside of me kept pushing me to never give up and keep me moving. I tended to slowly see where I was going and what I needed to do to keep moving forward, and to understand how and why my life was giving me a second chance to live and to make it right. I went along with hearing those business entrepreneurs give their speeches for me to understand them. I started by listening to many entrepreneurs that talked about having ambition, discipline, and purpose. You must have these three things to understand your grounds. Even venture capitalists are on all these platforms where anyone can Google information to learn and see how others have done it. You see, for everything you need as an entrepreneur or a businessperson, there are many tools out there for you to use to find yourself, to understand where you're going in life, and to know which door to open.

As you go out there and become the person you want to be, or even if you just want to start with how to give a speech to someone you think is going to be helped, just do it. Because as an entrepreneur, you are going to be asked a lot of questions, and you will be having lots of meetings and giving out lots of free speeches. As you take your steps to become an entrepreneur and start your own company, remember that you're writing a story, as well as telling your story to someone else so that they can aspire to be like you one day. Don't do it for the wrong reasons or for money. Do it because you love doing what you do and you want to be someone in life. Share that story with someone special or just be there for those kids who look up to you and really want their lives to be like yours someday.

Whatever you decide to do in life, remember that you're the key to what you give out to the world. You are the balance of your own life, as well as that person who will one day make everyone say, "That guy is one of the most important people that I ever met," or "That guy is one of the most important people that I ever had a great conversation with," and possibly even that you made their life worth living. Remember to believe in yourself and, whatever you do, it should come from the inside. See the world with your eyes, not with money or greed. Balance yourself with what you do, love your family and friends, make the most of your time, and be thankful for every moment in life that you can go out there and call yourself an entrepreneur, because you never know when it could be your last.

# XII

# THE GIFT YOU ARE GIVEN

# The Gift You Are Given

You're given the gift of life that is always fleeting with time. Sometimes, it can feel like you really don't know what is going on around you or in your head, but you seem to wonder if you do. You see, we are all in a time zone where we seem to think everything that we see or have been told is true. In your eyes, what you see and hear is what you believe. That is just a moment of light that you want it to be. But really, it's proof of life and meaning of a moment in time that is around you for a reason. Life is a beautiful thing that we really don't understand to this day. We love the feeling of it when we are drinking or having a good time, or just being around our loved ones. It feels good, right? But you don't really seem to understand that you are losing time every second of your life.

Really think about it for a moment. Does it really matter for you to go out and get into fights to prove to yourself that you're the boss or the MAN? It really doesn't matter at all because, at the end of the day, you are losing your life if you're living the fast way or if you are just living it with your family or loved ones. The way I see it, live to the fullest and think in motion. What I really mean by that is, when we wake up in the morning, we really don't think about our lives or what we are getting into that day. It's like being in LA traffic on the 405 – it's either going to move fast or slow; you just have to go along with it. But we don't really think about it because we just have to go and go.

Life is just like that. Yeah, you have to slow down and understand yourself before you run into a wall. We are like magnets; we really tend to grab everything that we think or see. If you really want to understand what I mean by all this, stop and think about your loved ones first, and just let everything sink in slowly. You will see you really don't have to be in 405 traffic at all; you can just be in your own lane. What I'm saying is you really don't have to be a part of anything if you don't want to be. You wanting to be a part of everything is going to make you not true to you.

Life is very important, and you should make the most of it when you can, because tomorrow you may not have the chance to live it the way you want to. The reason I'm telling you all this in my book is because I've been through these moments in my life, and by going through all this, I now understand my past and where I was coming from. You see, I'm a soul that understands life, time, and a moment of time. I'm a soul that wants to see you for you. I'm a soul that lives the way I want to live without hurting anyone. I'm a soul that loves you for you. I'm a soul for a reason, and I'm here to tell you that you should go out there and be who you really are and love those who matter the most in your life. Don't just sit there and wait for a moment to come. Go out there, grab it, and believe you are the one that can make a difference in someone's life.

# XIII

# KNOWLEDGE

# Knowledge

Knowledge is one of the important words in our lives that we don't really live by. We don't really pay attention to ourselves or what is really going on around us. That said, those of you who feel like "I-have-to-know-everything-about-every-word" will be happy to know that it really is possible, if we understand what we are trying to study or go after. We are given this great knowledge to understand not only what is going on around us, but also to understand ourselves to know where we are going and what it is that we really want from this word called knowledge.

We as people are all over the place, and we tend to fight over everything there is. All we do is want and want, but we don't really think about giving back to the world and to people. We are so into this greed of having everything that we want that money can buy, right? But if you die tomorrow or someday soon, are you planning to take everything with you? Right, like that is going to happen. We are designed to have as much knowledge as we can in order to understand what we can do with it or how to use it. The best thing in life is to understand why we are given the tools to be who we are and to give back as much as we can, because that is the key to living a happier life. Be as rich as you want to be, be happy as much as you want, and have what you want in life. Get it all, but do it with respect and dignity for others, because using the word of knowledge in the wrong way is not caring about others and only pretending to be good.

Knowledge is very important to all of us, especially to those who don't understand much and are trying to get there. That is why we as people are here to help. Those with more understanding and meaning of life and knowledge should help others to walk, talk, and see the world of opportunity that all of us really have by using knowledge and understanding it in every way. By seeing this power of knowledge and seeing things differently, you slow down to understand everything around you. Say thank you for everything that you have so far in life, and give back as much as you can by helping others to understand knowledge.

The key is to slow down, look around you, let time and everything pass you by, and let everything go fast as you can. Because you are in control of everything – your time, the way you are, and what is going on around you. Everything you want in life or think you want or wish you had, you've been asking for it and controlling it, even if you may not think about it or have only for a second. The understanding is that you did, and you are calling for it. Whatever you think or do in your life may close or open your doors to a greater life and knowledge that you may have never seen or understood until now. A word from me to you is to try to slow down in life; take as much time as you want. Know that it's always best to help others find themselves and make them understand who they really are. Understand knowledge and you understand yourself, so go out there and find yourself before it is too late to understand who you really are.

# XIV

# LEARNING RESPECT FROM DISRESPECT

# Learning Respect from Disrespect

Respect is one of the most powerful words in the world, because it really does move everyone around you, as well as makes you understand who you really are, where you come from, and where you are going. In life, we have moments where we tend to hate everyone or maybe we're just having a really bad day, but one thing to remember is to never try to disrespect anyone around you, no matter how bad of a day you're having. Respect comes from within you, and the purer your heart is, the more beautiful of a person you are going to be, no matter what is going on around you. Respect is what brings us all together as a person or as a family. Despite the reasons of others, all you must do is just be you, and make sure that you are the person who loves and understands the meaning of respect, so you as a leader can walk with people and show them the reason for and meaning of respect. Its reason doesn't matter where you're from, what color you are, or what religion you practice. Because at the end of the day, we are one, and together as family and friends, we are here to help others understand the meaning of respect and not to disrespect anyone of any level in life. <u>We as a people must come together and make things happen with respect to all people and bring them to love and understanding of life. We should not disrespect others or, as kids, disrespect our moms and dads or just family overall just because we may think family is wrong and don't understand where they are coming from.</u>

We as a people have the power of life, understanding, and the meaning of living the beautiful life God has given to all of us. We must come together and make it right before it's too late.

Disrespecting a person or anyone at all is where everything starts, such as fights, shooting, running away from family, or just talking back to your parents. It really doesn't go anywhere in life. All it does is make us do it repeatedly. We as a people of all religions need to come together as one and make this world a beautiful place for us to live in. Not just for ourselves, but for our kids and their kids to one day go out there and live life without getting disrespected by others that think they know everything because they have all the money in the world and think they are going to live forever by disrespecting others. Remember, a body at rest will always stay at rest in life, and it only moves by moving it. In life, we may own things like cars, houses, planes, or anything we may add on to our lives, but we all tend to forget one thing: we don't really own our bodies. We are just renting it, like a car or house until our time is up and the soul moves on to another body to start its life again.

So don't go out there and start fighting and disrespecting others because of their religion or color of their skin. Learn to respect and understand one another in life, and make the most of it where all of us can come together and help each other as a people and as humans of our times. Learn to respect others, give back, and help others to understand life and the meaning of living and making it right while we are still alive today. Make it count while we are still here, because there may not be a tomorrow at all for us to remember or understand.

# XV

# MOMENTS OF LOSING EVERYTHING

# Moments of Losing Everything

There will be moments in life where you will feel lost, even with everything that you have. Life is not easy for everyone, but you must make sure you make the most out of what you have and get the most out of what you really want. There will be days where you will feel like whatever you want may still not be good enough. Having everything doesn't really mean that you will really have everything that you want. It's better to see it in a way where you are happy and satisfied with what you already have, rather than sitting in the corner of a room and crying about it day and night. Moments of losing everything feel like no one is there to listen to you or to see you. It feels like you are alone in this world. In life, you must lose something to gain something better – something you never thought you could have. My advice to you is, if you're losing everything and you know that it is happening right in front of you, no matter how hard you try to stop it, let it be, and let go of everything that you are holding onto in life. Losing everything and then getting it back is a great feeling for the first time. It's like you had your first car or pet, but it's the feeling of being grateful for life, and you know that feeling this way is what you really wanted from beginning. Yes, losing everything sucks, but that is where we learn from our own mistakes of being so greedy, of wanting everything that we can't have or afford, but we are still willing to go after it and must show it off all the time and in everyone's face. If you are losing everything, or if you are thinking that you are losing everything around you, just stop for a moment, close your eyes for a minute, and don't think of anything. Just be in your zone and in the moment, and give yourself a break for everything that is going on around you. In life, it doesn't matter how old you are but it's what you do with it and what you make of it that counts. Open your eyes, let everything sink in time, and just restart from where you are. Forgive yourself for doing wrong or hurting someone. Walk along the path that you always wanted in life or go after that girl that you like so much. Ask her out, and see what happens. Remember, there is no wrong answer in life. It is what we make of it and how we see it that matter.

There is always an answer waiting for you somewhere. You just have to open your eyes and see it from the start. You are the answer to your own life's questions, and you have nothing to lose and everything to gain. So don't put yourself down, but be strong and be you, because there is always a way in life. Everything that you have done to feel right or wrong, you can make it better by just believing in yourself and making it happen. So, remember, whenever you feel like you are in losing mode or feeling that you are going to lose everything, just stop and think of the steps you took to get there, and that is always a way back to start from the beginning. You have nothing to lose in life but everything to gain. Everywhere you go, it's always you and has been you. Remember to just be yourself, and start over from whatever steps you're taking. Just be you.

# XVI
# THE WORDS

# The Words

Attraction is addiction, addiction turns to bad habits, and bad habits turn to hurting others. Understand yourself and be free. We are humans; mistakes will happen. We are neither right nor wrong. Learn to forgive yourself and others, and start over. The important part is to not get so attached to material things in life. Be thankful for what you have because you worked hard for it. Remember not to overthink it or overdo it, because everything you have can be gone tomorrow. Live everything in motion – meaning don't get attached to anything. Another important thing to remember is your loved ones. Everything else can be in motion. In life, it is your own thoughts that cause suffering. It's how you think and act that will become your path until you decide. Starting over is always the best way. But it's how you start over that will make you who you are. Don't change yourself because you don't fit in the group or because you're not so-called "cool". Be yourself, and the right people will join you.

Clear your mind, and just be true to you. Help others as much as you can to find yourself. Knowledge is two things: 1) reading books and understanding them, and 2) walking along in the real world and learning from life itself to understand what is important. Karma can be defined as doing something that you do not understand that will turn into wrongdoing, or karma can be doing well, understanding life, starting over by seeing things differently, and moving on with a happier life with your loved ones. How all this comes to understanding is by deep meditation of your own mind.

In life, it doesn't matter how old you are but what you do with your time here and what you make of it. That's what counts. Life is a canvas that is waiting for you to write on it with a pen or with a paintbrush. Be creative, and bring out the understanding of yourself and who you are from the inside. See the world as it is by seeing things in front of you differently. Time to time, you may feel down, or you may feel upset at not getting closer to your goals, but remember to take your time, understand everything around you. Being happy as you go along is what counts the most. For you to just get upset and give up is going to make you fall back in life. If you're walking, just keep walking and never look back. If you fall, get up and try again. Remember to never run away from your mistakes and always face them. It doesn't matter what the outcome is, just face it and keep moving forward.

We all have our ups and downs, but one thing I have learned is just keep moving forward despite everything. Whenever I'm down or feeling super bad or just don't feel like doing anything, I must keep moving, because to me there are no ifs. It just must happen. Either you have it inside of you or you don't. It is as simple as that. Life doesn't wait for you, and nor does time. If you have a dream, like you have always wanted to own a business or be a writer or just an artist, but you don't know where to start, don't think too much. Instead, map out a simple roadmap that doesn't have to be perfect, because starting somewhere is better than not starting at all.

# XVII

# WHEN OTHERS FEEL PITY FOR YOU

# When Others Feel Pity for You

When going after your dreams, the steps you must take, the pain you feel, the moments of put downs, and the path of not moving forward can all drive you nuts. I'm telling you that pitying someone can really backfire on you. Take my roadmap of success, for example. Understand that, for me, it was not easy to see or feel any of this from anyone. On the path of building my company, I met lots of people that could help me in every way possible. I mean, these people are family or close businesspeople that I knew for a long time.

I met with a lot of businesspeople and even family that could help me grow and who believed in me and was there for me… that is the meaning of family. Well, I had my share of meeting and giving advice to friends and family or just sharing my passion and my work. Remember, at the end of the day, you will feel quite a bit from your surroundings. When I started seeing all this was happening to me, I began to see how some family, friends, and businesspeople can really be in front of your face, feeling pity for you and your hard work. Their fake smiles, like words, will live forever. But to see all this, you must understand your surroundings and body language of others in every way. You see, as a business owner or founder, you must understand yourself and always be in control. Don't ever lose yourself in any emotions. Always understand that you are better inside and outside. Do the best you can to not feel fake pity for anyone, and be stronger from the inside and outside with a smile, because no one can break you. Only you can break you.

I have seen close friends feel pity for me, but at the end of the day, I keep my smile, because fighting over others' unprofessionalism is a waste of time, and not understanding the mind and body of your soul will break you in half. Be stronger from the inside and outside. Love your family and your real friends. Don't let others put you down. Build your roadmap to success. Who do you want to be loved by, and who do you want to love? Go after your steps to become the person you want to become, because only you and no one else can live out your dreams. I love when people don't believe me, because every time this has happened, I have always proven them wrong without saying any words, and there would be that day when they will say, "Wow, you really did do what you said you were going to do." You are Achilles versus Hector, David versus Goliath, and it doesn't matter how or what people think about you. If you have been put down, get up and fight for your words and dreams.

Go after your success, and make the most of it. Never let others put you down, and just give all you must give to win the fight. Don't let anyone feel pity for you, and if you see that they do, be strong and walk it off. Don't ever forget them, but always be yourself, and live to prove them wrong. Remember, you cannot give up once you start your dreams, and you cannot back down. You are a one-of-a-kind person from inside out. You have the right to love. Live the way you want, but do it the right way to give back. Feel free to understand yourself and the people around you, and go after your dreams to live your life the way you've envisioned it. Never let anyone stop you.

# XVIII

# WAYS OF FUNDING WITHOUT GETTING FUNDED

# Ways of Funding Without Getting Funded

Finding business funding or capital can be very hard. Do you have bad credit? Have you tried getting funding in many different ways, but it was still very hard to get? That is okay, because I had the same experience. I lost everything, and I still managed to find a way to get funding for my business. This was through a second job. It feels good to make things happen when you feel you can't have or get funding for your own business. Believe me, there is always a way to get your work out there. At first, you may feel out of place for not having the right kind of funding. It may drive you nuts, because it will take time for you to find funding based on your experiences.

The best part about all this is that you must have an entrepreneurial spirit or, without it, you will get lost. Most people won't understand where you are coming from as a person, but as an entrepreneur, you will always find a way to succeed, because it's not something that you just decided to do today or yesterday. This is something that you had inside of you since the day you were born. The point here is you will feel out of balance or not see faster growth in your business, but you are strong. Don't give up in anything that you do. Yes, investors want to see charts or even projections of your business outline for you to get funded. Yes, banks are not going to play that easy or just want to give you funding. Yes, some people count on their family to give them funding prior to giving them a percentage of the company.

Now, remember, I'm not trying to step you off your game here, but family business can be a bad idea, according to chart history. Keeping your business to yourself and working on your vision to grow the way you want is the best way to go, so don't think about putting yourself out there faster than you should. Keep working hard at what you do, and never worry about what others are thinking about you or saying about you. You are the only person that can understand your business and your vision about where you want to take it. Don't let anyone rush you in what you do, because it's your time and your hard work. You're depending on yourself and the way you are in understanding the business, and helping your family by working two jobs to support them shows that you don't give up easily... But continue to fight, and keep fighting for what you believe in. Be willing to take your business where you want it to go. Love what you do, and do what you love. Never say never, and never let anyone put you down. Your dream is to be someone. Never give up. Be who you are, and make something happen. Keep going.

# XIX

# WORKING ON A VERY HIGH LEVEL

# Working on a Very High Level

Everything comes down to one thing – never stop working on a very high level. What I mean by that is being responsible for the things you do, the people you meet, the meetings you have, and working all day and late nights, but still manage to get up in the morning at 5 am and think about what you do. Life is full of phases, and you will see them as you go. The best advice is to be yourself. Never give up, and never say never. Time will pass by, and you will be able to say, "'Yes, I'm really happy with what I have done." Surround yourself with the friends and family that really love you and are happy for you to live your dreams day by day. Love every moment of your life. Be free to do what you love, and be free to help others around you to create a world by design that really matters to you. Be understanding, and be able to see the people that really look up to you as a person that can create success. So never stop believing. Never stop working. Go after your dreams. Deliver that meeting to investors and venture capitalists, and don't knock on the door. Instead, break it down, and say, "I'm here to stay, whether you like it or not. This is my idea, and I will be successful."

I really hope you enjoy this book, as I came a long way and fought for where I stand. Remember, at the end of the day, you are just you, and everything will come to you eventually. I wish that all of you are successful in what you do.

# XX

# SELF-AWARENESS / BE PATIENT

# Self-Awareness / Be Patient

To those who really don't understand self-awareness, it is one of the most important things in life. It is self-understanding of everything that is going on around you. Being in that moment of a movement has no <u>limits of time</u> because, in reality, there is <u>no such thing as time</u>. Self-awareness is taking a careful step towards your success. You don't just walk blindly. Self-awareness is also a success of patience. Patience is everything in life. It is how you understand patience that will lead your mind and body to self-awareness, to a greater and happier life. You see, 90% of people really don't understand how to be patient, because they don't have it in them. Pushing people around and disrespecting others will only make your name less important or reduce it to the level of a 5-minutes-of-success person that you already are now. Because the point here is, if you're being a major ass to everyone, there will come a time when everything will come crashing down on you and in your life. It may even come to a point where your own family and friends will despise you because of your actions and behavior. However, this is that moment of self-awareness and being patient that I'm talking about for you to just be you.

    Still don't understand? That's okay. Let's make this simple. Have you ever witnessed a situation where someone is asking for help and everyone just walks by them, thinking they are so cool because they think nothing can ever go wrong in their perfect little worlds of make-believe and not caring about anyone, until that beautiful day comes where everything is not supposed to go wrong with their perfect little life, but it does anyway? The next thing you know, they are the ones asking for help but everyone just keeps walking right by them, because there was a time when they were the ones who walked by someone in need, and now, they are the ones in need. That's where patience plays a big role in life – through understanding, giving back, helping, and most importantly, having self-awareness. If you don't understand self-awareness and being patient, then you never will.

# XXI

## SELF-MOTIVATION

# Self-Motivation

Here, I'm going to talk about how I motivated myself and believed in my company. Remember – having hope, believing in yourself, and being motivated is the start to success, and you're going to get there. You must always be clear-minded, and you must be aware that you have lots of things in your mind throwing you off at any given moment. <u>What you think in your mind is what you're going to do and attract.</u> You must have a point of view and understanding of what you want and how you are going to lay your path down that road. As a founder/CEO and a person that wants to succeed in life, this is what I do every morning. I lay out my path first to see how I want to walk it.

I wake up every morning around 5:30, lay my blue yoga mat down on the floor, and stretch. Once I'm done stretching for about thirty minutes, I sit down with my legs crossed, like they sometimes do in yoga class. I think of myself as an assassin. Why? You must be disciplined, on time, have a clear mind, and be aware of your body and soul. I close my eyes and just be myself. I absorb the energy around me, and give myself another round of fifteen minutes to clear my mind even more. Then, when I'm done with my yoga, I move on to thirty minutes of any workout of my choice. After my workout, I sit on the mat, close my eyes, clear my mind, and be thankful for another day.

I call this the soul of silence. I start by thanking God for giving me this great life and for the things I have in my life, as well as blessing me with strength. I'm very lucky to have everything I have in life. When I open my eyes, I see what I have. It's a blessing to me, and I thank God for everything that He has given me and for opening roads of opportunities for me to walk. When I look at others out there, and I see that most people don't have everything that I have, it makes me feel thankful for what I have. I don't ask for more. I go out and give back, for it is in giving back that you will be rewarded. Don't be greedy, but be thankful.

This is how I start my mornings – with a clear mind, alone time, a grateful heart, and a smile on my face while I'm getting up from my blue yoga mat and getting ready for my business day. You see what I'm doing there? I'm balancing my time and my mind for the next part of my day.

# XXII

# FEELING OF BEING ALONE

# Feeling of Being Alone

Being alone in life to some may seem like unfeeling, happy moments that others may never understand without asking themselves why. Feeling alone or being alone in life, sometimes, can be a great thing, because it gives you time to regroup and understand yourself better, as well as gives you time to understand the world better. It gives you time to see how the world is so beautiful in so many ways that most people can't see, because they are clearly blind or distracted. It gives you time to see, think, and feel the moment that you are in. It gives you time to be thankful for what you have or had, and appreciate the moments that this world has given us humans to build our business, from time spent at home and in train stations and coffee shops. It gives you time to forgive yourself and forgive others who have done you harm. You see, there is nothing too important in life at that moment and at the end of the day, because time is everything, my friends. <u>We cannot take back time that is wasted. What we as humans have done in the past that causes us to be alone, it has been for a reason – for you to understand the movement of reality and the self-understanding of why you are alone.</u> Yes, feeling alone can be scary at times because you may feel unloved by others. Or you just may feel it's better for you because you like to be alone and be in control of your time and space.

    Being alone to me is a beautiful thing because there comes a time where I really do feel like I have no friends at all. Take that first step to go outside and start walking on a beautiful, rainy day with a smile on your face. Go to that coffee shop for a Chai tea to go, so you can enjoy being alone and being away from others to find beautiful nature outside, where you can think, forgive, and do better to bring yourself back to where you were before in life. Being alone gives you self-awareness and understanding of you as a person, a leader, a self-starter, or just plain old you and whatever you may be thinking as you go along that path in beautiful nature, trying to find yourself and your purpose of being alive with a soul and a body that is just a rental and may be gone before its time one day. Being alone is not a bad thing at all. It shows how you are and what brings you to life while being you at those moments. Being alone is beautiful, and everything just stops around you to enjoy for that one special day. In others' eyes, being alone is a judgmental thought of you not having anyone or having anything at all for that matter. It's that moment when everyone is in your space and they really can't understand themselves but will be ready to judge *you* right away, even without understanding themselves first, or understanding their mistakes from being a human. So, if you find yourself being alone, believe me. I understand. Everything happens for a reason that we may not understand. Sometimes, we do not want to try at all; we just run away from it. Take my advice: being alone will sometimes bring you to life from who you are today and will bring you closer to your future by understanding the lessons that come from the time of being alone.

# XXIII

# WON'T MATTER IF I LEFT

# Won't Matter if I Left

What if I was gone one day? Would anyone care? I have these thoughts in my head, these feelings in my heart, and I see the concerns of others and how everyone moves with no meaning besides their own. What if I was gone today or tomorrow? Would it even shake the ground around me? There are moments when you start to question yourself. When you are in a moment of silence, standing still, and everyone and everything moves around you. Think of it as time lapsing around you where there is nonstop, moving time that most of us won't understand when we are gone.

As you go along with the feeling of being gone one day, there is a point in your life where you run into those important understandings of life and it does give you a purpose to fight to live another day, before you're gone. We have the most beautiful thing called life where, for most of us, we really don't tend to value what life can offer us. Maybe it would be different if we just take some time to regroup. Having the time for yourself to regroup will help you work through moments in your life that you have gone through, starting at the time of your birth. Life does go backwards from the day you were born. The timeline of your life and the steps you take to make it happen – meaning every breath of air and the light of the sun and the sound of the waterfall and the feeling of being alive – just brings the purpose of life in a bit, in a way that you cannot ask for and in more ways than one. Life is so beautiful that most of us really do take it for granted, but when you get time to stop and think and see, you tend to feel so great that nothing else matters.

# XXIV

# PHOTOGRAPHY & WRITING

# Photography & Writing

Moments of life get me going as a photographer and writer. This is where one morning, I may get up out of bed, brush my teeth, take a warm or cold shower, get ready afterwards with a nice Trask – dark brown chukka boots – with dark blue jeans, and a navy V-neck T-shirt and top it off with a dark coffee-colored leather jacket. Afterwards, I make myself some hot Chai tea with a sumptuous breakfast of over easy eggs and a side of toast with avocado and a few newspapers that I may read as I go along with my day. Then, I start my car and randomly pick a place where I want to go. I go hiking with my notebook and my camera, so I can take that moment in my day to create a moment that I write about.

The moments I feel and the moments I see in nature are for me to live and capture them as I see everything in front of me. The moment of silence yet keeps me smiling, brings happiness to me, and makes me feel grateful. And at that moment, I feel thankful for life. The beautiful fall leaves, the wet path of the park, the singing birds that surround me as I walk along, capturing those beautiful moments of life with my camera and enjoying every minute of it. I come across to a point where I must sit, and as I am overlooking the beautiful ocean, I take out my pen and notebook that I have, and I start to write about what I feel and what I am seeing as a writer from being in that moment. I really like these types of moments and the feeling when I am sometimes alone, so I really get to understand life better and I have the time to get away from all the drama that is out there. These types of life moments and the feeling that comes with being part of the beautiful nature that is given to us really helps to understand living life from being a part of it.

These moments do give me time and a place to think and feel, to forgive and to start over from my past mistakes, and to get a chance to be alive again, as I see how life comes in many forms. The light of the sun, the whisper of the birds, and the language of the oceans and all the living things around me – even the tree that I'm sitting next to – are all experiencing the same moments that I am with my pen and notebook. As I write and think, I may come across moments of good feelings and maybe decide to call someone to say, "I love you" or "I'm sorry," and try to restart a beautiful life that I still may have the power to change. As I leave that beautiful park of nature, I look back one more time, and I feel alive, happy, and thankful for me and for the great photographer and writer that I really am.

Thank You

*THE END*